First edition November 2024

Book design by Rhonda Shaw
Map by Demarje' Adair

ISBN (paperback) 9798218551551
ISBN (ebook) 9798218551551

Dedication

To my husband, Jaspierre Smith, thank you for being an inspiring role model for our children. It fills me with joy to see them observe you and aspire to emulate your greatness. Thank you for choosing me to embark on this journey of life together.

Jasper and Jace were sitting on the couch, barely able to contain their excitement. Jasper kept checking the clock every few minutes. "Mom, where is Dad? I really want him to come home now," Jasper asked eagerly.

"He should be home any minute now. Just be patient, it won't be long," Mom reassured them. Jasper slumped in his seat and mumbled, "But when is soon?"

Suddenly, Jasper and Jace heard the familiar jingle of Dad's keys at the door. Their faces lit up as they jumped up and ran to the door.

DAD'S HOME!!!

"Hey Dad, we have something super exciting to tell you," Jace screamed as they both rushed to Dad. "I can't wait to hear your exciting news," Dad said with a smile, placing his bags on the floor and joining them on the couch.

"Dad, guess what we want to be when we grow up," Jasper said with a mischievous grin.

"Are you going to be firefighters?" guessed Dad.

Jasper and Jace shook their heads, and Jace added, "But we will be just as brave!"

"Will you be doctors?" Dad tried again.

"No, but we'll make sure everyone feels well every day," Jasper replied.

Scratching his head, Dad said, "So you will be brave and keep people feeling well every day. Hmmm!"

"I got it!" exclaimed Dad. "You want to be police officers."

Jasper and Jace shook their heads again. "But we will keep people safe," Jace explained with a grin.

Dad walked in a circle thinking, as the boys waited eagerly, he pondered.

"So you'll be brave, care for people, and keep them safe. A teacher, perhaps?"

The boys giggled. "Not quite, but we will help people learn things," Jasper replied.

Dad leaned back on the couch, looking thoughtful. "You'll teach, be brave, care for people, and keep them safe. Boys, I'm stumped. What do you want to be when you grow up?"

"YOU!" both boys exclaimed with
a sparkle in their eyes.

"We want to be just like you when we grow up, Dad. You are brave and make sure we are well every day," Jasper said earnestly. Jace hugged his dad, "You keep us safe and teach us every day."

WE LOVE YOU!

I LOVE YOU TOO!!

Milton Keynes UK
Ingram Content Group UK Ltd.
UKHW051158251124
451531UK00002B/10